LEWIS
LATIMER

LEWIS LATIMER

*Winifred Latimer Norman
and Lily Patterson*

CHELSEA HOUSE PUBLISHERS
New York   Philadelphia

Chelsea House Publishers

Editorial Director Richard Rennert
Executive Managing Editor Karyn Gullen Browne
Executive Editor Sean Dolan
Copy Chief Robin James
Picture Editor Adrian G. Allen
Art Director Robert Mitchell
Manufacturing Director Gerald Levine
Systems Manager Lindsey Ottman
Production Coordinator Marie Claire Cebrián-Ume

Black Americans of Achievement
Senior Editor Richard Rennert

Staff for LEWIS LATIMER
Editorial Assistant Joy Sanchez
Designer John Infantino
Picture Researcher Wendy P. Wills
Cover Illustrator Bradford Brown

5 7 9 8 6 4

Library of Congress Cataloging-in-Publication Data
Norman, Winifred Latimer
    Lewis Latimer/Winifred Latimer Norman and Lily Patterson.
      p. cm.—(Black Americans of achievement)
    Includes bibliographical references and index.
    Summary: Discusses the inventor's career, life, and times.
    ISBN   0-7910-1977-2
            0-7910-1978-0 (paper)
    1. Latimer, Lewis Howard, 1848–1928—Juvenile literature.
2. Afro-American inventors—United States—Biography—Juvenile
literature. [1. Latimer, Lewis Howard, 1848–1928. 2. Inventors.
3. Afro-Americans—Biography.]
I. Patterson, Lily. II. Title. III. Series.
T40.L37N67 1993   93-185
609.2—dc20   CIP
[B]   AC

Frontispiece: *Lewis Latimer (front row)
attends the 1918 meeting that marked the
founding of the Edison Pioneers, an
annual gathering of inventor Thomas
Edison's chief employees.*

CONTENTS

BLACK AMERICANS OF ACHIEVEMENT

HENRY AARON
baseball great

KAREEM ABDUL-JABBAR
basketball great

MUHAMMAD ALI
heavyweight champion

RICHARD ALLEN
*religious leader and
social activist*

MAYA ANGELOU
author

LOUIS ARMSTRONG
musician

ARTHUR ASHE
tennis great

JOSEPHINE BAKER
entertainer

JAMES BALDWIN
author

BENJAMIN BANNEKER
scientist and mathematician

AMIRI BARAKA
poet and playwright

COUNT BASIE
bandleader and composer

ROMARE BEARDEN
artist

JAMES BECKWOURTH
frontiersman

MARY MCLEOD BETHUNE
educator

GEORGE WASHINGTON
CARVER
botanist

CHARLES CHESNUTT
author

BILL COSBY
entertainer

PAUL CUFFE
merchant and abolitionist

MILES DAVIS
musician

FATHER DIVINE
religious leader

FREDERICK DOUGLASS
abolitionist editor

CHARLES DREW
physician

W. E. B. DU BOIS
scholar and activist

PAUL LAURENCE DUNBAR
poet

DUKE ELLINGTON
bandleader and composer

RALPH ELLISON
author

JULIUS ERVING
basketball great

LOUIS FARRAKHAN
political activist

ELLA FITZGERALD
singer

MARCUS GARVEY
black nationalist leader

JOSH GIBSON
baseball great

WHOOPI GOLDBERG
entertainer

ALEX HALEY
author

PRINCE HALL
social reformer

JIMI HENDRIX
musician

MATTHEW HENSON
explorer

BILLIE HOLIDAY
singer

LENA HORNE
entertainer

WHITNEY HOUSTON
singer and actress

LANGSTON HUGHES
poet

ZORA NEALE HURSTON
author

JESSE JACKSON
civil-rights leader and politician

MICHAEL JACKSON
entertainer

JACK JOHNSON *heavyweight champion*	RONALD MCNAIR *astronaut*	COLIN POWELL *military leader*	MADAM C. J. WALKER *entrepreneur*
MAGIC JOHNSON *basketball great*	MALCOLM X *militant black leader*	PAUL ROBESON *singer and actor*	BOOKER T. WASHINGTON *educator*
SCOTT JOPLIN *composer*	BOB MARLEY *musician*	JACKIE ROBINSON *baseball great*	DENZEL WASHINGTON *actor*
BARBARA JORDAN *politician*	THURGOOD MARSHALL *Supreme Court justice*	DIANA ROSS *entertainer*	OPRAH WINFREY *entertainer*
MICHAEL JORDAN *basketball great*	TONI MORRISON *author*	WILL SMITH *actor*	TIGER WOODS *golf star*
CORETTA SCOTT KING *civil-rights leader*	ELIJAH MUHAMMAD *religious leader*	CLARENCE THOMAS *Supreme Court justice*	RICHARD WRIGHT *author*
MARTIN LUTHER KING, JR. *civil-rights leader*	EDDIE MURPHY *entertainer*	SOJOURNER TRUTH *antislavery activist*	
LEWIS LATIMER *scientist*	JESSE OWENS *champion athlete*	HARRIET TUBMAN *antislavery activist*	
SPIKE LEE *filmmaker*	SATCHEL PAIGE *baseball great*	NAT TURNER *slave revolt leader*	
CARL LEWIS *champion athlete*	CHARLIE PARKER *musician*	DENMARK VESEY *slave revolt leader*	
JOE LOUIS *heavyweight champion*	ROSA PARKS *civil-rights leader*	ALICE WALKER *author*	

ON ACHIEVEMENT

Coretta Scott King

Before you begin this book, I hope you will ask yourself what the word *excellence* means to you. I think that it's a question we should all ask, and keep asking as we grow older and change. Because the truest answer to it should never change. When you think of excellence, perhaps you think of success at work; or of becoming wealthy; or meeting the right person, getting married, and having a good family life.

Those important goals are worth striving for, but there is a better way to look at excellence. As Martin Luther King, Jr., said in one of his last sermons, "I want you to be first in love. I want you to be first in moral excellence. I want you to be first in generosity. If you want to be important, wonderful. If you want to be great, wonderful. But recognize that he who is greatest among you shall be your servant."

My husband, Martin Luther King, Jr., knew that the true meaning of achievement is service. When I met him, in 1952, he was already ordained as a Baptist preacher and was working toward a doctoral degree at Boston University. I was studying at the New England Conservatory and dreamed of accomplishments in music. We married a year later, and after I graduated the following year we moved to Montgomery, Alabama. We didn't know it then, but our notions of achievement were about to undergo a dramatic change.

You may have read or heard about what happened next. What began with the boycott of a local bus line grew into a national movement, and by the time he was assassinated in 1968 my husband had fashioned a black movement powerful enough to shatter forever the practice of racial segregation. What you may not have read about is where he got his method for resisting injustice without compromising his religious beliefs.

He adopted the strategy of nonviolence from a man of a different race, who lived in a different country, and even practiced a different religion. The man was Mahatma Gandhi, the great leader of India, who devoted his life to serving humanity in the spirit of love and nonviolence. It was in these principles that Martin discovered his method for social reform. More than anything else, those two principles were the key to his achievements.

This book is about black Americans who served society through the excellence of their achievements. It forms a part of the rich history of black men and women in America—a history of stunning accomplishments in every field of human endeavor, from literature and art to science, industry, education, diplomacy, athletics, jurisprudence, even polar exploration.

Not all of the people in this history had the same ideals, but I think you will find something that all of them had in common. Like Martin Luther King, Jr., they all decided to become "drum majors" and serve humanity. In that principle—whether it was expressed in books, inventions, or song—they found something outside themselves to use as a goal and a guide. Something that showed them a way to serve others, instead of only living for themselves.

Reading the stories of these courageous men and women not only helps us discover the principles that we will use to guide our own lives but also teaches us about our black heritage and about America itself. It is crucial for us to know the heroes and heroines of our history and to realize that the price we paid in our struggle for equality in America was dear. But we must also understand that we have gotten as far as we have partly because America's democratic system and ideals made it possible.

We are still struggling with racism and prejudice. But the great men and women in this series are a tribute to the spirit of our democratic ideals and the system in which they have flourished. And that makes their stories special and worth knowing.

1

THE DRAFTSMAN

ALEXANDER GRAHAM BELL developed an interest in sound at a young age. Born in 1847 in Edinburgh, Scotland, he boasted a wonderful ear for music and soon showed great promise as a pianist. But he was fascinated by science as well as music, and shortly after he entered his teens he turned his attention to the study of spoken sounds.

Bell's parents played pivotal roles in shaping his interest in this field of study. His mother, who had encouraged young Alexander's interest in music, was nearly deaf; she could hear only when aided by a rubber tube placed against her ear. His father was a highly regarded public speaker and speech teacher; to help his wife and other deaf people who had difficulty in speaking to learn how to talk, he devised a system of pictorial images that he called visible speech.

The images used in visible speech show a person how to position his or her tongue, teeth, and lips to form specific sounds. Alexander soon became very familiar with this system. And when he moved to the bustling city of Boston, Massachusetts, in 1871, he became a teacher, using his father's system to instruct deaf children how to speak.

Thanks to visible speech, it did not take long for Bell to make a name for himself in Boston. Within a year of his arrival, he was tutoring deaf students in

A highly accomplished engineer, Lewis Latimer was a pioneer in the development of electricity. He worked with two of the leading inventors of his time, Alexander Graham Bell and Thomas Edison, to help bring about the 20th century's technological revolution.

11

visible speech, running a school to train instructors in the system, and giving lectures on speech at the local universities. And in what little spare time he had, he was trying to elevate the power of human communication by inventing a device that could send multiple messages simultaneously over a single telegraph wire to a receiver.

In 1874, Bell decided to alter the aim of this device. Rather than send electrical waves over a telegraph wire in the form of Morse code, he wanted to create a machine that could convert people's voices into electrical waves and transmit them in the same way that the telegraph worked. To aid him in the project, he turned to 20-year-old Thomas Watson, an electronics whiz and master craftsman who worked in a nearby electrical shop.

Because both Bell and Watson kept busy schedules, they were forced to perform their experiments in their spare time, mostly at night. First in the attic of the electric shop where Watson worked and then in a set of rooms that the two men rented, they made one attempt after another to send people's voices to a receiver. Bell, with his dark eyes and jet-black hair, was the picture of intensity.

At last, on June 2, 1875, Bell enjoyed a significant breakthrough. His device transmitted a sound that was more than just an electric pulse. The sound rose and fell and varied in pitch, just as a person's voice did. Bell began to believe that in just a few months he would successfully realize his dream of electronically transmitting voices from one place to another.

But it was one thing to invent the device that would become known as the telephone. Getting the invention patented by the U.S. government was an entirely different matter. A patent is a written promise from the government that secures for an inventor the right to make, use, or sell his or her invention exclusively for a certain number of years and gives

the inventor the right to prevent others from making, using, or selling that invention. Bell knew that it was urgent to get his device registered at the U.S. Patent Office in Washington, D.C., as soon as possible. The longer that it took him to have the plans for the telephone drafted and patented, the greater became the risk that someone else would register a similar

This photograph of inventor Alexander Graham Bell was taken in 1876, around the time he had his plans for the telephone patented. Latimer, who worked less than a block away from Bell in Boston, executed the drawings for the plans.

invention. Then Bell would lose all ownership rights to the invention.

To draw up the plans for the telephone, Bell turned to Lewis Latimer, a draftsman who worked for Crosby and Gould, a firm of patent lawyers located less than a block away. At age 27, Latimer was just a year younger than Bell. But the draftsman looked nothing like Bell; Latimer had large eyes, a winsome smile, and—unlike most men who held office jobs in the late 19th century—light brown skin.

A Massachusetts native, Latimer had settled in Boston a decade earlier, after serving in the U.S. Navy aboard the USS *Massasoit* during the Civil War. Following his honorable discharge from the military,

"Mr. Watson, come here. I want you!" were the first words Alexander Graham Bell sent over the two components of his telephone, a transmitter and a receiver. The call to his assistant took place on March 10, 1876, three days after Bell received a patent for his invention.

he was hired by Crosby and Gould as an office boy. His starting salary was three dollars a week.

From such humble beginnings, Latimer became a highly accomplished draftsman. He began his study of the art of mechanical drawing by watching a draftsman at the office. Then he purchased some secondhand drawing tools and practiced on his own. Eventually, people at the firm recognized Latimer's drawing talent and made him a draftsman. After that, he worked his way up to head draftsman—quite a feat for a young man whose parents had been born into slavery.

By the time Bell contacted him, Latimer had already received a patent for an invention. In 1874, he had teamed up with W. C. Brown to invent a more functional bathroom than the one then being used on trains. Latimer had received a patent certificate for the invention, "Improvement of Water Closets," on February 10, and his experience in obtaining the

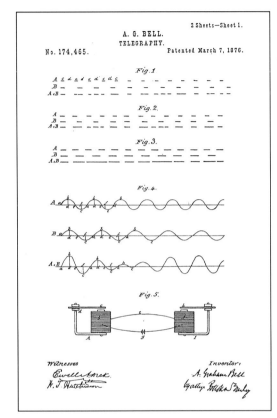

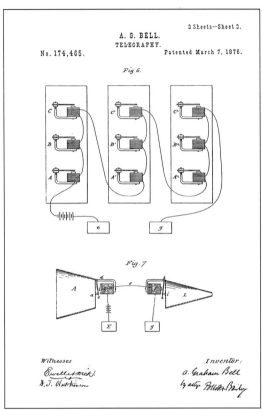

Latimer made these drawings for Alexander Graham Bell's patent application for "new and useful Improvements in Telegraphy," which was Bell's description of the "method of, and apparatus for, transmitting two or more telegraphic signals simultaneously along a single wire." According to some sources, Latimer not only provided the drawings but helped Bell write the application for the invention that became known as the telephone.

patent taught him exactly how to go about getting one for Bell.

According to some historians, Latimer not only drafted the plans for Bell's telephone but helped with the wording of the patent application. In any event, Latimer worked long hours with Bell and helped him prepare the plans for the telephone. "I was obliged to stay at the office until nine P.M.," Latimer recalled of his work with Bell, "when he was free from his night classes, to get my instructions from him, as to how I was to make the drawings for the application for a patent upon the telephone."

Bell filed an application with the U.S. Patent Office on February 14, 1876. As it turned out, several hours later, another inventor, Elisha Gray, submitted his own plans for a telephone. But Gray was too late.

Bell—with Latimer's help—had won the race. On March 7, Bell received the patent for the telephone. And just three days later, Bell uttered those historic words, the first ever sent and received via the telephone: "Mr. Watson, come here. I want you!"

True to his personality, the quiet and unassuming Latimer never boasted about the role that he played in this drama. Nevertheless, in the years that followed, the brilliance of his genius would become evident. The Latimer name had already been etched into American history by his father, a runaway slave who served as a focal point of the abolitionist movement; Lewis Latimer would see to it that his family's name would never be forgotten. **

2

"LATIMER SHALL GO FREE!"

———— •❦• ————

LEWIS HOWARD LATIMER was born on September 4, 1848, in Chelsea, a Massachusetts town located next to Boston. Situated between the Chelsea and Mystic rivers, Chelsea had initially been settled as a trading post. But its population grew over the years, and in 1857 it was incorporated as a city.

At the time of Lewis's birth, Boston was widely acknowledged as the cultural and intellectual center of the United States. Yet for young Lewis, daily life was not filled with scenes of ease and artistry but of struggle and hardship. His world had been shaped by circumstances that had occurred long before his birth. Indeed, these events had already made the Latimer name a part of American history.

Lewis's paternal grandfather was Mitchell Latimer, a plantation owner and slaveholder in Norfolk, Virginia, who sired a son with one of his slaves, Margaret Olmstead, in the early 1800s. Their boy, George Latimer, grew up as a slave on the plantation. Like many children of white slaveholders and their black slaves, he was granted one or two special favors. During his childhood, he was spared the harsh life of a field slave and was employed as a house servant. And when he got older and developed into a handsome, athletic young man, he was allowed to hire himself out and to keep the wages that he earned.

George Latimer, Lewis's father, grew up in slavery in Virginia before escaping in 1842 to Massachusetts. There the fugitive slave became a pivotal figure in the abolitionist movement.

William Lloyd Garrison was editor of the nation's leading abolitionist newspaper, The Liberator, *and cofounder of the influential American Anti-Slavery Society. An uncompromising abolitionist, he crusaded for George Latimer to be freed from prison after slave hunters captured the fugitive slave in Massachusetts on October 18, 1842.*

Despite his comparatively privileged existence as a slave, George was not happy with his lot in life. Ever since he had been small, his strongest desire was to be free. He later said that he "thought frequently of running away even when . . . little," and he made several unsuccessful attempts at escape. He tried to flee the plantation although he knew that an escape attempt might lead to freedom but could also lead to death.

In early 1842, George married 20-year-old Rebecca Smith, who belonged to another slaveholder. By then, George had become the legal property of James Gray, a storekeeper. Gray allowed George to visit his wife only at night, after he had finished his work. He was then required to return home before sunrise.

As soon as George and Rebecca learned that they were going to become parents, they decided to escape and make their way north. Both of them knew that unless they reached a free state, their child would be born a slave and could be taken away from them by their owners. George bided his time, saving the money that he had earned while working at other jobs. Finally, he had enough cash to buy two railroad tickets.

On October 4, 1842, Rebecca and George Latimer slipped onto a steamer at Norfolk and hid for nine hours in the darkness of the ship's hold. When the vessel reached Baltimore, they used their railroad tickets to travel to New York. Being fair skinned, George posed as a Virginia planter, and Rebecca played the role of his servant. Four tense and exhausting days of travel later, the courageous couple reached the free state of Massachusetts. George chose to go by the name of Latimer, vowing that in freedom he would bring honor to the name of his father.

But George and Rebecca were not out of danger. As fugitive slaves, they could be recaptured and transported back to Virginia. There, they could face a variety of punishments. They might be beaten, sold to another slaver, or put to death.

Not long after the fugitive slaves arrived in Boston, George was recognized by William Carpenter, who had worked for the runaway slave's owner back in Virginia. Carpenter immediately contacted Gray, who had advertised in the *Norfolk Beacon* for the return of his fugitive slave. The notice read: "He is about five feet three or four inches high, about twenty-four years of age, his complexion is bright yellow, he is of compact, well made frame, and is rather silent and slow-spoken."

Rebecca's owner had also advertised in the *Norfolk Beacon* for the return of his runaway slave: "Run away from the subscriber last evening, Negro woman Rebecca in the company (as is supposed) with her husband, George Latimer, belonging to James B. Gray of this place. She is twenty years of age, dark mulatto,

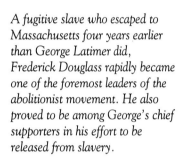

A fugitive slave who escaped to Massachusetts four years earlier than George Latimer did, Frederick Douglass rapidly became one of the foremost leaders of the abolitionist movement. He also proved to be among George's chief supporters in his effort to be released from slavery.

copper colored . . . self-possessed and easy in her manner when addressed. . . . All persons are hereby cautioned against harboring said slave."

Gray came to Boston on October 18 and had George arrested. Meanwhile, Rebecca was whisked away to a safe hiding place. According to later reports, she stayed "at the house of a friendly abolitionist on High Street."

The news of George's arrest spread quickly through Boston's black community. The day after he was grabbed by the police, more than 200 former slaves assembled outside the Leverett Street Jail, where he was being held. They created a spectacle by forming a human wall around the building to prevent anyone from spiriting George Latimer back to Virginia. A trio of Boston's most distinguished attorneys—Charles Ellis, Amos Merrill, and Samuel Sewell—promptly agreed to represent him at his trial. All three were staunch opponents of slavery.

Latimer also had an ally in William Lloyd Garrison, who stood at the forefront of the abolitionist movement. In 1831, Garrison began publishing *The Liberator*, a newspaper that boldly trumpeted his position on slavery. "He that is with the slaveholder is against the slave," Garrison stated. "He that is with the slave is against the slaveholder." *The Liberator* soon became the nation's leading antislavery newspaper, and by 1840 about 200,000 Americans belonged to at least one of the nearly 2,000 antislavery organizations that existed across the United States.

The Liberator was among several newspapers to announce that on October 30, a public meeting to discuss George Latimer's imprisonment and his right to freedom would be held at Boston's historic Faneuil Hall. During the American Revolution, many town meetings had been held at the hall in protest of British rule. Faneuil Hall was also the site of the Boston Massacre, an incident in 1770 that saw an-

A large public building in Boston that served as headquarters for the patriots during the American Revolution, Faneuil Hall was the site of the Boston Massacre, an incident in which fugitive slave Crispus Attucks became the first man to die in the American colonies' fight for independence from Great Britain. More than 70 years later, on October 30, 1842, a public meeting was held at the historic hall to discuss George Latimer's imprisonment and his right to freedom.

THE LATIMER JOURNAL, AND NORTH STAR.

" Star of the North, I look to thee   While on I press: for well I know   Thy light and truth shall set me free."

VOL. .I.   BOSTON, WEDNESDAY, NOVEMBER 23, 1842.   NO. 5.

THE LATIMER JOURNAL.

TERMS.—One cent a number, tri-weekly. A liberal discount to newsmen and boys. Advertisements (at discretion) one cent a line.

Edited by an association of gentlemen, and published every Monday, Wednesday and Friday mornings, at No. 15 State Street. It is not connected with the Courier.

Wm. White & H. P. Lewis, Printers,
Minot's Building, Spring Lane.

My Fatherland. By Koerner.

Where is my Fatherland?
Where fires of spirits high were glowing,
Where flower crowns for the fair were growing,
Where manly hearts, glad freedom knowing,
Burned for all holy things to stand—
There was my Fatherland !

Why weeps my Fatherland ?
Because he people's rulers, quaking
At mad oppression's wrath o nbreaking,
Crouch, all their holy vows forsaking,
Because her cries no ear command,—
This weeps my Fatherland !

Whom calls my Fatherland ?
Though stricken deep, yet n t despairing—
She calls aloud with steadfast bearing,
For Freedom,—for a saviour-daring,
To stay the avenger's scourging hand—
These calls my Fatherland !

What will my Fatherland ?
Her foe's slave host she yet will shatter,
Will from her soil the blood-hounds scatter,

own liberties. *We have endeavored not to say anything about Southern oppressors, but we here plainly tell them that they must never DARE come to Massachusetts to prostrate our laws to support their own institutions, as they have done in the present case.* The Latimer case was a test case, and its result has been a triumphant one. We rejoice in its bloodless termination. We commenced our career in turmoil and threatened bloodshed, we terminate in peace and freedom.

To our readers we again say adieu, and to our correspondents we give our sincerest thanks. A number of communications still remain on file, and will remain for the present, unless any one wishes them in manuscript. They will remain as a *corps de reserve* with which to bear down upon any enemy that shall appear upon our borders.

Subscribers and Outstanding Accounts.

Will every one who has subscribed for our Journal, send in immediately, the amount of his subscription? The burden of payment falls on two. Come then to their help.

A Voice from Danvers, New Mills.

A full and respectable meeting of the citizens of this place, was held in the Engine room, Nov. 17th, to take into consideration

dence, insulted the memories of the revolutionary heroes, violated God's laws, treated with contempt the teachings of Jesus Christ, given her professedly free soil as hunting ground to that detested human being, the human blood-hound, and invited the slave owners to seize upon our sons and daughters, and carry them into slavery, and made herself a fair mark for the scorn and contempt of the whole civilized world.

Resolved, That the late decision of the Supreme Court, by which the soil of Massachusetts is made hunting ground for slave holders, ho wever it may accord with the letter of the Constitution of the United States, is directly opposed to the teachings both of the old and new Testament—hostile to the best interests of humanity, and subversive of the rights of freemen.

Voted, To publish the doings of this meeting in the Latimer Journal.
J. P. HARRIMAN, Chairman.
A. R. PORTER, Sec'y.
Danvers, New Mills, Nov. 17, 1842.

COMMUNICATIONS.

For the Latimer Journal.

Latimer is Free !

Latimer is free ! What mighty significance is there in these three words ! Let them sound from the green hills of Berkshire, from whence so lately came the prophecy of freedom, and which has already been fulfilled. Let them sound through our whole broad State ! Latimer is free ! The

Grand Convention of Freemen !

At the Marlboro' Chapel, Saturday, Nov. 12.

The meeting was called to order by Dr Henry Ingersoll Bowditch, and organized by the choice of Francis Jackson, of Boston, as President, and William Bassett, of Lynn, as Vice President. In the absence of Francis Jackson, William Bassett took the chair, and the organization of the meeting was completed by the choice of H. I. Bowditch and M. W. Chap an as Secretaries, and Ellis Gray Loring, Charles Lenox Remond, J. T. Raymond, J. M. Spear, Henry W Williams, Joshua Leavitt and Caroline Weston, as a business committee.

The following resolutions were adopted with the warmest expressions of satisfaction in them:

1. Resolved, That we welcome, this day, this meeting of freemen, to say to this State, and to this country, that which fills their hearts:—that the freedom of George Latimer is an epoch in the cause of American liberty, and that we hail it as one in a long series of events which will end only in the universal freedom of our beloved country.

2. Resolved, Tha we most respectfully call upon the people of this State, for such an expression of their deep love of freedom, that they will emphatically call upon their

---

The Latimer Journal and North Star, *issued three times a week, was founded by abolitionists to publicize George Latimer's imprisonment and his fight for freedom. "We have endeavored not to say anything about Southern oppressors," the November 23, 1842, edition of the paper said in support of Latimer, "but we here plainly tell them that they must never DARE come to Massachusetts to prostrate our laws to support their institutions, as they have done in the present case."*

other fugitive slave, Crispus Attucks, become the first man to die in the American colonies' fight for independence from Great Britain. Accordingly, to the people of Boston, Faneuil Hall was popularly known as the Cradle of Liberty.

As word of George's plight spread, numerous abolitionists became involved in the attempt to get him released. Among them were John Greenleaf Whittier, a poet whose antislavery verse was published in *The Liberator*. In honor of George, Whittier penned the inspirational "Virginia to Massachusetts," which featured the lines: "No slave-hunt in our borders, no pirate on our strand! / No fetters in the Bay State, no slave upon our land!"

Frederick Douglass was another towering figure in the antislavery movement who spoke out on George's behalf. A fugitive slave who had escaped to Massachusetts in 1838, Douglass became an agent of the Massachusetts Anti-Slavery Society and a powerful lecturer on abolition. Remembering his own daring

CAUTION!!

COLORED PEOPLE

OF BOSTON, ONE & ALL,

You are hereby respectfully CAUTIONED and advised, to avoid conversing with the

Watchmen and Police Officers of Boston,

For since the recent ORDER OF THE MAYOR & ALDERMEN, they are empowered to act as

KIDNAPPERS

AND

Slave Catchers,

And they have already been actually employed in KIDNAPPING, CATCHING, AND KEEPING SLAVES. Therefore, if you value your LIBERTY, and the *Welfare of the Fugitives* among you, *Shun* them in every possible manner, as so many *HOUNDS* on the track of the most unfortunate of your race.

Keep a Sharp Look Out for KIDNAPPERS, and have TOP EYE open.

APRIL 24, 1851.

A poster in Boston warns blacks to be on the lookout for slave catchers hunting for fugitive slaves in the area. Notices such as this one caused George Latimer to fear for his family's safety even after he gained his freedom in 1842.

escape from slavery only four years earlier, he corresponded with Garrison, and Douglass's letter became one of his first pieces of writing to be published.

As popular support for George Latimer increased, the *Liberator* urged the public to maintain its interest in the case and to "be vigilant, firm, and uncompromising, friends of freedom." A large number of citizens heeded these words, and an excited crowd attended the October 30 meeting at Faneuil Hall. After the meeting, the slogan "Latimer shall go free!" became a familiar cry on the Boston streets.

Not only did the newspapers pick up the refrain, but the Latimer case inspired the birth of a new publication, the *Latimer Journal and North Star*. Edited by Dr. Henry Bowditch, William Channing, and

Frederick Cabot, the first issue came out during the furor of George's trial. The paper contained firsthand accounts of the case and included an interview with Latimer himself. When asked what might happen to him should he be forced to return to Virginia, he said he would probably be "beaten and whipped nine lashes . . . perhaps to be washed in pickle afterward."

The days leading to George's trial were filled with suspense and gossip. One rumor, which said that a ship was already being held in Boston Harbor to take him back to Virginia, was countered by another, which declared that the vessel's captain would refuse to return him to the slave state.

Finally, Chief Justice Lemuel Shaw of the Massachusetts Supreme Court issued a ruling that confirmed George as the personal property of James Gray. At the same time, two petitions, signed by many abolitionists, requested that the fugitive be set free. While these petitions were being considered, Latimer was returned to his jail cell. Sewell, fearing that George's owner might try to recapture him by force, advised Latimer to scream as loud as he could if anyone should try to take him from jail. His cries would alert the group of former slaves standing guard around the jail to come to his rescue.

Realizing that under the court's ruling George was still his owner's legal property, a group of abolitionists began to negotiate to purchase Latimer from Gray. Bowditch offered to pay $650 for Latimer. Gray agreed to the figure, and George was released. But now that Latimer was a free man, Bowditch did not think that it was necessary to pay Gray the money.

The Reverend Samuel Caldwell, minister of the Tremont Temple Baptist Society, was not taking any chances. He raised $400, handed it over to Gray, and the matter was settled. Exactly one month after he had been arrested, George Latimer was legally a free man. And with that news, the cry of "He is free! He is free!" rang through the city's streets.

George was promptly reunited with Rebecca, whose whereabouts, according to the former slave, "were never disclosed." Moreover, after he received his freedom, "her master made no further trouble." To make matters even sweeter, the Latimers' first child, George, Jr., was born soon after the trial. And he was born free, as his parents had dreamed. ❧

3

"BOUND OUT"

A MAN OF action, George Latimer decided to help out other fugitive slaves by preventing them from experiencing what he did. Immediately after his release from jail, George later wrote, he "began to attend anti-slavery conventions and appeal for signatures to the famous 'Latimer' petitions." These petitions, also known as the Grand Petitions, called for lawmakers to pass bills that would prevent the capture of fugitive slaves. More than 100,000 citizens signed these petitions, which were presented to Congress by John Quincy Adams, who had become a congressman after serving from 1825 to 1829 as the sixth president of the United States.

The Latimer petitions failed to inspire Congress to protect the rights of fugitive slaves. But they did lead to the Massachusetts Personal Liberty Law, which made it illegal for state officials to help capture a runaway slave.

Through it all, George remained a celebrity. Both the *Salem Observer* and *The Liberator* reported on an event at which "George Latimer, the lion himself, was present. His appearance caused a sensation among the audience. . . . At the close of the meeting, by the request of several present, Latimer stood in front of the rostrum, that those who wished might pass along and shake hands with him, as is the

An aerial view of Boston taken in 1860, shortly before Lewis Latimer entered his teens. Born in nearby Chelsea, he resided in Boston until he was in his early thirties.

29

custom when the president and other distinguished men receive the attention and civilities of the sovereign people."

Unfortunately for George, his well-documented escape and release from prison did not lead to a prosperous livelihood. Freedom for a black man in the mid-19th century posed the same challenge that slavery did. Daily existence was a matter of survival.

Seeking to make ends meet, George moved his family from one place to another over the next few years. And by the end of 1848, the Latimer family consisted of four children. In addition to their son George, Jr., George and Rebecca also had a daughter, Margaret, another son, William, and an infant boy, Lewis.

Lewis would recall his early years in a journal that he kept. Written in the third person, as though he were a character in a drama, he noted: "His first recollection of a home was a house on Oswego Street a street which ran east from Harrison Avenue in Boston. . . . Lewis remained here but a short time and then moved a little farther uptown to Orange Lane, a strictly Irish neighborhood. . . . From Orange Lane the Latimers moved to the west end of Boston near Massachusetts General Hospital and after a short time here, went to live on Phillips St. then known as Southac St., a strictly colored neighborhood. They were located here for a number of years."

In addition to struggling to earn money, George felt it necessary to move his family so often because of the Fugitive Slave Law of 1850. This piece of federal legislation declared that any black accused of being a runaway could be brought before a federal judge or a special commissioner. Denied a jury trial or even the right to testify on his or her own behalf, the alleged fugitive could easily be returned to slavery. All that the law required was a sworn statement from a white individual who claimed to be the black person's owner. The law also provided heavy penalties for anyone who helped the slave escape.

Because Rebecca still fell into the category of being a fugitive slave, George lessened the danger to his family by moving frequently. Probably one of the reasons why the Latimers resided at Phillips Street "for a number of years" was that their neighbors, Lewis and Harriet Hayden, operated a station on the Underground Railroad, a loose network of people willing to hide runaway slaves in their homes and "conduct" them to the next "station," or safe house.

Freedom was clearly a subject that preoccupied George. His feelings about slavery ran so deep that in his spare time he occasionally wrote poetry about black liberation.

> With thy pure dews and rain,
> Wash out, O God, the stains
> From Africa's shore;
> And while her palm trees bud,
> Let not her children's blood
> With her broad Niger's flood . . .
> Will thou not Lord, at last
> From thine own image cast
> Away all cords,
> But that of love which brings
> Man, from his wanderings
> Back to the King of Kings,
> Lord of Lords!

When he was not writing poetry, George had to help make ends meet, and to do that he enlisted the aid of his three sons. During the 19th century, it was not unusual for boys to begin working before they reached their teens—and Lewis was no exception to this way of life. When he was not helping out his father, Lewis attended Phillips Grammar School. He was such a good student that he even skipped a grade, and it soon became obvious to all who knew him that he loved to read, write, and draw—skills that he would rely on heavily as he got older.

A 19th-century engraving of a barbershop run by blacks. During his youth, Latimer worked in his father's barbershop on Cambridge Street, helping him clean the shaving brushes, sweep the floor, and put things in order after the workday was done.

Lewis, however, spent much of his childhood working at his father's barbershop on Cambridge Street, eagerly helping George clean the shaving brushes, sweep the floor, and put things in order after the workday was done. His father, Lewis wrote in his journal, also "worked in a store on Washington Street hanging paper." Remaining at his father's side night after night, the young boy "became quite expert as a paper hanger." Lewis greatly enjoyed his father's company, and years later he would recall the time that they spent together with great affection.

As a result, Lewis's world was turned upside down in 1858, when his father disappeared without a trace. To this day, George's departure from his family remains a mystery. Some historians believed that he feared he was endangering his family's safety. Just one year earlier, the U.S. Supreme Court had ruled on a case involving Dred Scott, a Missouri slave whose master had taken him to the free territory of Minnesota and then back to the slave state of Missouri. Claiming that residence in free territory had made him a free man, Scott sued for freedom from his master. When the state supreme court decided against Scott, his abolitionist lawyers took his case to the U.S. Supreme Court.

After hearing lengthy arguments on both sides of the question, Chief Justice Roger B. Taney issued the Court's majority opinion. Scott, said Taney, was not a citizen and had no right to sue in a federal court. The Constitution had created a white man's government, and blacks, "beings of an inferior order," wrote Taney, had "no rights which a white man was bound to respect."

Perhaps George felt that his celebrated status as a runaway slave would make him an obvious target for slave catchers. Because he did not have any official papers to prove that he was free, slave hunters might try to spirit him back to Virginia. And so he would be placing his wife and children in danger every day that he remained with them.

In any case, with her husband gone, Rebecca Latimer had to find some way of supporting her family. During the mid-19th century, it was common for children to be "bound out" as apprentices. Under such an arrangement, they received vocational training—and, sometimes, meager pay. In his journal, Lewis noted that "his two brothers were sent to a state institution then known as the Farm School, from where they were bound out. George was sent to a farmer and William to a hotel keeper in Springfield. Margaret, Lewis's sister, was taken by a friend and Lewis remained in his mother's home until she got a chance to go to sea as a stewardess . . . [and] arranged to send him to the Farm School."

Prior to being sent to the Farm School, Lewis sold copies of *The Liberator*, reading the articles and

Isaac Wright, a prominent Boston lawyer, hired Latimer as an office boy during the early 1860s. Lewis continued to work for Wright's firm up until 1864, when he became a soldier in the Civil War.

learning about the growing antislavery movement whenever he got the chance. At the Farm School, he felt much like a slave and wanted desperately to come home. Along with his brother William, he plotted an escape. One day, they and a friend stole away from the school. They made their way to Boston by hiding in railroad cars and reached the city after several days of traveling.

Upon being reunited with her two sons, Rebecca Latimer, Lewis recalled, "sheltered them until they could go to work such as boys could do." He waited on tables and did housework for a family in Roxbury. At the age of 13, he landed a job as an office boy for Isaac Wright, a prominent lawyer. Lewis would continue to work there for the next several years.

Meanwhile, slaveholders in the South were calling ever more loudly for enforcement of the Fugitive

Slave Law and for punishment of anyone who broke it. In November 1860, Abraham Lincoln was elected president of the United States. Upset that an abolitionist was stepping into the nation's highest elected office, South Carolina seceded from the Union and raised the specter of a civil war between the slave and free states.

In February 1861, the remaining six states of the Deep South—Alabama, Florida, Georgia, Louisiana, Mississippi, and Texas—withdrew from the Union to form the Confederate States of America. On April 12, Confederate troops opened fire on the federal garrison at Fort Sumter in Charleston, South Carolina. The soldiers in the fort surrendered the next day, and the nation went to war. ☙

4

"MAY I DO SOME DRAWINGS FOR YOU?"

❧

A LARGE CROWD gathered in the Boston Tremont Temple on the night of January 1, 1863. The air buzzed with excitement and anticipation. Frederick Douglass, the former slave who had crusaded for George Latimer's freedom more than 20 years earlier, kept spirits high as the anxious group awaited the news. When it finally came, cries and shouts filled the temple. President Abraham Lincoln had signed the Emancipation Proclamation late that afternoon, ending slavery in the South. The more than 3 million black men, women, and children who had been slaves "are and henceforth shall be free," the Proclamation decreed. "The year of jubilee is come," Douglass proclaimed.

When the Civil War began, Lincoln had prohibited blacks from serving in the Union army because he feared that their presence would anger most of the white soldiers and cause tension in the ranks. But as the war dragged on, Massachusetts governor John Andrews declared that northerners no longer cared whether their soldiers traced their roots "from the banks of the Thames or the banks of the Senegal." The Union simply needed more troops. Lincoln

The Emancipation Proclamation, signed by President Abraham Lincoln on January 1, 1863, paved the way for Latimer and other blacks to enroll in the nation's military. Lincoln's edict marked the first time in history that the law of the land granted blacks equal treatment with whites.

A Civil War–era poster published by the Supervisory Committee for Recruiting Colored Regiments. Latimer was among the more than 185,000 black soldiers who took part in the Union war effort.

agreed that more soldiers were needed, and in 1862 he authorized the arming and training of blacks.

At first, black soldiers were assigned to segregated units under the command of whites and were given

menial tasks to perform. It was not until mid-1863, when the 54th Massachusetts Regiment, an all-black infantry unit—commanded, however, by a white officer, Captain Robert Gould Shaw—was sent into

The USS Massasoit *was the gunboat on which Latimer served during the latter stages of the Civil War. The steamer took part in the North Atlantic Blockading Squadron, blocking the path of Confederate vessels while protecting Union ships voyaging between New York and Virginia.*

battle, that important use was made of black troops. By the war's end, the U.S. Bureau of Colored Troops had recruited and trained more than 185,000 black soldiers, with more than 38,000 of them dying in the war.

Lewis Latimer and his two brothers were among the many blacks who welcomed the opportunity to bring an end to slavery. George, Jr., enlisted in the 29th Connecticut Army Regiment, and William joined the navy. Lewis, however, had a problem. Barely 16 years old, he was too young to enlist.

Faced with the prospect of being denied a chance to serve his country, Lewis lied about how old he was so that he could meet the minimum age requirement. On September 16, 1864, he was assigned as a landsman (seaman) to the USS *Massasoit*, a gunboat that was part of the North Atlantic Blockading Squadron. Among the *Massasoit*'s duties were to protect Union ships voyaging between New York and Hampton Roads, Virginia, and to block the path of Confederate vessels. The gunboat wound up taking part in the Battle of Howellett's House and carrying vital messages to Union general William Tecumseh Sherman in North Carolina.

At the end of the war, the *Massasoit* returned to Boston, and Latimer received an honorable discharge from the navy on July 3, 1865. Soon after, he wrote in his journal, he "went into housekeeping in a couple of rooms on Phillips Street" with his mother. Boston by then was experiencing a major change in its population. Shiploads of immigrants—many from Ireland, where a potato famine was causing starvation and death—were arriving at the port, and competition for jobs was keen.

Even though Lincoln had issued the Emancipation Proclamation two years earlier, blacks were still not being treated by whites as equal citizens. Many employers remained hesitant about hiring former slaves. Even when they were hired, most employers paid blacks lower wages than they paid whites for doing the same work.

In his journal, Latimer described the day that he "finally" found work. He wrote that "a colored girl who took care of the office of some lady copyists was asked to recommend a colored boy as office boy, one 'with a taste for drawing.'" Latimer fit the bill. He had more than "a taste" for drawing—he had an absolute passion for it. He applied for the job, which was at Crosby and Gould, a firm of patent lawyers, and was hired. The salary was three dollars a week, which was low but on a par with the wages being paid to blacks at that time.

The firm of Crosby and Gould did a brisk business. With the Civil War over—it came to an end three months prior to Latimer's discharge from the navy—people were beginning to invent and explore new uses of technology as never before. Many applications for patents were requested.

Every day, Latimer saw the draftsmen at Crosby and Gould turn the applicants' sketches of their inventions into scientific drawings that could be presented to the U.S. Patent Office in Washington, D.C. He was eager to learn this trade, and he said of

This certificate documents Latimer's discharge from the U.S. Navy on July 3, 1865.

himself in his journal, "He watched to find out what tools were used, then he went to a secondhand book store and got a book on drawing."

The eager office boy saved money from his small salary until he had enough to buy a few of these drawing tools. Then he watched one of the draftsmen perform at his board day after day, read the book on drawing, and practiced drawing after he returned home at night. After a while, Latimer wrote in his journal, he began to feel that he was "thoroughly. . . master" of his art.

One day, after months of careful observation and unfailing study, Latimer felt that the time had arrived to show off his newly developed skills. He approached the head draftsman at Crosby and Gould and asked him politely, "May I do some drawings for you?"

The surprised draftsman laughed at the earnest young man but eventually decided to give Latimer an opportunity to show what he could do. Latimer later wrote that the draftsman was amazed to see "that Lewis was a real draftsman, so he let him do some of his work from time to time and one day the boss saw him at work and was so pleased that he let him work everyday and gradually raised his wages."

Latimer wound up working for Crosby and Gould for 11 years. During that span, he rose from the position of office boy at 3 dollars a week to head draftsman at 20 dollars—a good wage for those times. (His wages as head draftsman were, however, still 5 dollars less than the salary received by white draftsmen.)

As head draftsman, Latimer supervised putting the final touches on working models of inventions before they were submitted to the U.S. Patent Office. He was also asked to assume the responsibility of managing the company whenever his employer, George Wilson Gregory, was not at the office.

A trio of second-floor signs (on the building at right) reads "J. B. Crosby, Solicitor of Patents." Latimer joined this firm of patent lawyers as an office boy shortly after he was discharged from the Union navy.

While Latimer was working as a draftsman, he discovered another interest that competed with drawing for his attention. Her name was Mary Wilson, and she came from Fall River, Massachusetts, a seaport town about 50 miles from Boston. The couple was married on September 20, 1873.

Although Latimer did not discuss in his journal how he met Mary Wilson, he spent a considerable amount of time reflecting on the love that he felt for her. Like his father, he enjoyed writing poetry, and he penned his poem "Ebon Venus" as a tribute to his wife.

> Let others boast of maidens fair,
> Of eyes blue and golden hair,
> My heart, like needle ever true,
> Turns to the maid of ebon hue.
> I love her form of matchless grace.
> The dark brown beauty of her face.

Massachusetts native Mary Wilson wedded Latimer on September 20, 1873. They were married for more than 50 years and had two daughters, Emma Jeannette and Louise Rebecca.

Her lips that speak of love's delight.
Her eyes that gleam as stars at night.
O'er marble Venus let them rage.
Who set the fashions of the Age.
Each to his taste; but as for me
My Venus shall be ebony.

During his time with Crosby and Gould, Latimer became quite expert at drawing models for new inventions. Eventually, however, he discovered that he not only wanted to help patent the inventions of others but wanted to develop some of his own ideas. In 1874, this desire became a reality, when he and W. C. Brown became the co-inventors of an improvement in the quality of the water closets, or bathrooms, that were used on trains. With his first patent,

Latimer joined the ranks of the post–Civil War scientific pioneers.

Latimer was someone who liked to broaden his horizons. If a person learned one skill, he believed, that made it easier to learn another. "You can help shape your future," he maintained, "by taking advantage of present opportunities no matter how small nor how few they may be. Good habits and good manners are powerful means of advancement that rarely fail to bring reward. Think of your future and plan for it the best you can. But now and then, pause and ask yourself, 'What can I do today?'" 🙿

Experiment No. 1.   Feby 13 1880
                              5-3

                         Chas Batchelor

small horseshoe

5

AN ILLUMINATING
INVENTION

·ᐧᐧ·

NEITHER LEWIS LATIMER nor Alexander
Graham Bell could possibly have imagined how
important their collaboration in the mid-1870s would
prove for future generations. For how could they have
known that the telephone—the invention that re-
sulted from their joint effort—would become indis-
pensable to people all over the world? As far as
Latimer was concerned, drafting the plans for the
telephone simply meant a chance to work for the first
time with an electrical device other than the electrical railroad signals that he drew at Crosby and Gould.

In time, however, Latimer would establish an
"Electrical Recollections" section in his journal. His
work with Bell led to a fascination with electricity,
and this interest would last for the rest of his life. It
would also help to bring the world many more
significant inventions.

Latimer remained at Crosby and Gould for another two years after his association with Bell ended
in 1876. He worked for a while with School Street
patent lawyer Joseph Adams and at a pattern shop at
the Esterbrook Iron Foundry in South Boston. But

*A sketch of a light bulb drawn
by the inventor Thomas Edison.
He was issued a patent for an
incandescent light bulb on
April 22, 1879.*

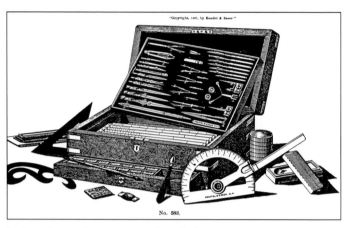

"Copyright, 1887, by Keuffel & Esser."

No. 583.

An engraving from the 1880s of a draftsman's tools of the trade. Latimer had mastered the art of mechanical drawing by watching draftsmen practice their profession.

before long, Latimer realized that it was time to move on. Boston was in the middle of an economic depression, and there was little work to be found.

Encouraged by his sister, Margaret, who had moved to Bridgeport, Connecticut, with her husband, Augustus Hawley, Latimer and his wife relocated to the bustling city on the Long Island Sound at the end of 1879. In his journal, he describes Bridgeport as being "perfectly alive with inventors . . . it would be next to impossible to throw a stone into any company of men gathered anywhere about in the street without hitting one." The thriving city was also home to many items of worldwide importance, including sewing machines and corsets.

While Latimer looked for work in the drafting field, he earned a living as a paperhanger. A short time later, he found work as a draftsman at the Follandsbee Machine Shop. It was during his stint at this shop that he met a man who would change the direction of his life.

Hiram Maxim was the founder and chief electrician for the U.S. Electric Lighting Company. Born in Maine, Maxim came from a family of famous inventors. His family had developed a series of weapons used in warfare, including the Maxim guns that became standard weapons in the United States and Britain.

Hiram Maxim (holding one of his many inventions, the Maxim gun) emerged as Thomas Edison's chief rival in the field of incandescent lighting. Latimer worked for both men, joining Maxim's employ in 1879 and Edison's four years later.

One day in 1879, Maxim stopped by the Follandsbee Machine Shop. He watched the slender, light brown–skinned man working skillfully on a drawing for some time.

"Hello," Maxim said to Latimer after a while. "I never saw a colored man making drawings. Where did you learn?"

Just as Latimer had told the astonished draftsman at Crosby and Gould how he had developed his drawing talent, so, in his usual polite, cordial manner, he explained to Maxim how he had mastered the art of drafting. Maxim was so impressed that Latimer had been the head draftsman at Crosby and Gould, a company with an excellent reputation and one he

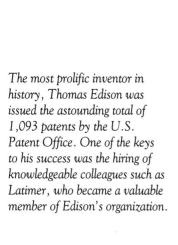

The most prolific inventor in history, Thomas Edison was issued the astounding total of 1,093 patents by the U.S. Patent Office. One of the keys to his success was the hiring of knowledgeable colleagues such as Latimer, who became a valuable member of Edison's organization.

himself had once worked at, that he hired Latimer on the spot. "Within a week from the time we first met," Latimer remembered, "I was installed in Mr. Maxim's office busily following my vocation of mechanical draughtsman, and acquainting myself with every brand of electric incandescent light construction and operation."

About a year before Latimer joined Maxim's company, the inventor Thomas Alva Edison had received a patent for an electric light bulb. There was a growing demand from businesses and private home owners for this new kind of lighting device, which yielded much brighter light than that given off by gas and oil lamps and candles.

This new type of lighting device, however, was not more practical than the much older forms of light. Edison's light bulb was made of glass, with a carbon wire filament inside that was constructed of paper, bamboo, or thread. The filaments were made by burning the cellulose found in these materials inside an airless bulb. Without air, the cellulose would break down, leaving the carbon, which would act as the filament in the light. When an electric current was sent through the wire into the bulb, the filament would become hot enough to glow.

The problem with Edison's light was that the filament lasted only a short time—a few days at the most. It was difficult and very expensive to keep replacing light bulbs. In order to make electric light available to the general public, a filament that would burn for a longer period of time had to be found. Experts all over the world in the field of electricity, knowing electric light was the wave of the future and a great money-making prospect, worked frantically to solve the problem.

While working for Maxim, Latimer learned first-hand everything that there was to know about this new field, the seeds of his fascination with electricity having been planted during the time that he worked with Bell on the telephone. Soon, he too joined the likes of Edison and Maxim in the race to find a solution to the filament problem and to create a longer lasting electric light.

In his typically organized manner, Latimer meticulously studied the problem and tried to make the puzzle pieces fit. He conducted hundreds of experiments with different methods and materials. It was important not only to make the electric light glow longer but also to use materials that would be cheap enough for the average consumer to afford.

Finally, after days and nights of trial and error, Latimer succeeded in solving the mystery. His method combined previous manufacturing techniques with several new materials that allowed the

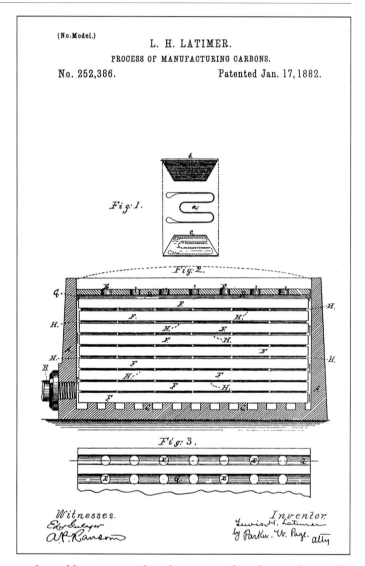

(No.Model.)

L. H. LATIMER.

PROCESS OF MANUFACTURING CARBONS.

No. 252,386.

Patented Jan. 17, 1882.

These drawings by Latimer accompanied his January 17, 1882, patent for "carbonizing the conductors for incandescent lamps, though it is equally applicable to the manufacture of delicate sheets or strips of dense and tough carbon designed for any purpose whatever." Latimer's discovery revolutionized the field of incandescent lighting because carbon filaments made electric lights more affordable and longer lasting.

carbon filaments to last longer and to be made much more inexpensively. Latimer's procedure involved stuffing blanks, or shapes, of such fibrous materials as wood or paper into small cardboard envelopes and then exposing them to extremely high temperatures in an airless environment. He discovered that by coating the inside of the envelopes with a substance that kept them from sticking, or encasing the blanks between two strips of tissue paper, he could keep the blanks from welding to the envelopes.

It was the cardboard envelopes that made Latimer's invention different from existing filaments—and that made it work so well. The envelopes expanded and contracted at the same rate as the wood or paper from which the blanks were made. This prevented the carbons from becoming misshapen or broken, as they had in the method used before Latimer made his discovery.

Even more important, Latimer's method allowed for the first time the easy—and cheap—production of carbon filaments. At last, average families and businesses could afford to illuminate their homes and workplaces with the brilliance of electricity—and to live by lights that would last. ◖◗

6

BRANCHING OUT

❦

LEWIS LATIMER'S METHOD for manufacturing cheap, long-lasting light bulb filaments opened the door to a new era of artificial lighting. The days of huddling near a dim, flickering oil or gas lamp were soon over. Electric lights sprang up in homes, businesses, streets, and everywhere else that people assembled.

For a long time, however, many accounts of the technological revolution that brought electric lighting to the world failed to even mention Latimer's contributions. Sadly, one reason for this seems to have been the color of Latimer's skin. Less than 20 years after the abolition of slavery, most whites were unwilling to accept that the son of a former slave could equal or surpass the efforts of his white competitors.

Another reason for Latimer's obscurity was that when he created his long-lasting carbon filaments he was working for the U.S. Electric Lighting Company, which received the credit for Latimer's inventions— and reaped all the profits. Failing to receive much glory has generally been the lot of the salaried researcher. But Latimer's employer, Hiram Maxim, was known to be especially quick to steal the credit for other people's ideas.

Although Latimer perfected the carbon filament and its connection to the metallic wire in a lamp base, the entire fixture became known as the Maxim lamp, after Latimer's employer. Hiram Maxim even saw to it that the carbon filaments in the lamp (near the top of the light bulb) were twisted into the shape of the letter M to represent his own surname's initial.

An 1880 engraving from Frank Leslie's Illustrated Newspaper depicts "The Wizard of Electricity—Thomas A. Edison experimenting with carbonized paper for his system of electric light, at his laboratory, Menlo Park.—from sketches by our special artist." Yet it was Latimer, not Edison, who finally developed a way of producing carbon filaments inexpensively.

One inventor who also worked for Maxim, Professor William Sawyer, said in a newspaper interview, "I know Mr. Maxim very well, and while he is beyond a doubt one of the best mechanical engineers in this country, I have no hesitation in saying that in his last attempt at electric lighting he has made a wholesale appropriation of other people's property." Sawyer added that Maxim had not only stolen his own ideas, but that "several times he had the effrontery to claim to others before my face ideas given by me." Sawyer also accused Maxim of using without permission ideas that Thomas Alva Edison had patented.

Edison had secured the first patent for electric lighting and was still the leader in the field. Although Sawyer did not like Edison personally, he said, "I have respect for a man that travels on his own merits," a pointed reference to Maxim's less scrupulous business tactics.

As Latimer's employer, Maxim did have the legal right to the patents that Latimer developed while working for U.S. Electric Lighting Company. Maxim not only kept the profits generated by Latimer's ideas but took all the credit. One of his most important products, which incorporated at least two of Latimer's inventions, he named the Maxim electric lamp.

The Maxim lamp was the first to use Latimer's carbon filaments, for which he submitted a patent application on February 19, 1881. Before Latimer had even received this patent—the patent office was swamped by eager inventors at the time, and his application was not granted until January 17, 1882— he had already applied for another patent. With a coworker, Joseph V. Nichols, Latimer had found a new way to connect carbon filaments to the base of a lamp. This technique was also first exploited in the so-called Maxim lamp.

Perhaps the ultimate irony was that Maxim insisted that the filaments in his Maxim lamps be shaped into the letter M. It was Latimer's method of making carbon filaments, which kept the carbons from curling up under the intense heat required for their production, that made it possible to control the filaments' shape. But it was Maxim's initial, not Latimer's, that was proudly displayed in glowing light to all who purchased the lamp.

The hardworking Latimer was not one to complain. Just a few months after patenting his process for making carbon filaments, Latimer and John Tregoning received another patent for an improvement in a different type of electric lamp that used no filaments at all.

This invention was a new kind of base for electric arc lamps. Arc lamps produce light by sending an electric current across a gap between two carbon rods

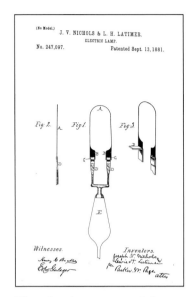

These drawings accompanied a patent granted to Latimer and a colleague, Joseph Nichols, on September 13, 1881, for "new and useful Improvements in Incandescent Electric Lamps." The improvements included a better way of connecting Latimer's invention of a carbon filament to the metallic wires in a lamp.

in the form of a continuous spark. Although quite bright, arc lamps are also very noisy, and for this reason they never became popular as a method of interior lighting. They made excellent streetlights, however, and were also used for years in searchlights and film projectors.

Latimer's knowledge of arc lights and the standard incandescent lights made him one of the foremost experts in the industry. He aided in the construction of the first electric plants in Philadelphia, Montreal, and New York City. Latimer also supervised the installation of lights and wiring in railroad stations, streets, and buildings in these three cities and directed a large staff in the production of carbon filaments. The buildings that he brought electric lights to included the offices of the *Philadelphia Ledger* newspaper, and the Equitable Building and the Union League Club in New York. But his work in Montreal was the most impressive.

The city of Montreal is in a French-speaking part of Canada, so none of the workmen whom Latimer supervised spoke English. Yet he had to teach them to perform precise, technical operations that were totally new to them. By studying at night, Latimer learned enough French to write detailed instructions for his assistants. "This was my nightly lesson," he wrote in his journal. "My day was spent climbing telegraph poles and locating arc lamps on them with the assistance of my laborers who seemed much impressed with my effort to speak their native language."

Because Latimer was the only person at the U.S. Electric Lighting Company who understood every aspect of producing the new light bulbs, when Maxim decided to open a factory in London, England, he sent Latimer to London to oversee the enterprise. With his wife, Mary, Lewis boarded a boat for England in spring of 1882. Both were excited about

Early electric arc lamps illuminate Chestnut Street in Philadelphia. Latimer helped develop a new kind of base for the arc lamp, which could produce much more light than the standard incandescent lamp.

Sporting a bowler, Latimer strolls through a park in London, where he was sent by Hiram Maxim in 1882 to oversee the opening of a light bulb factory. Latimer's work for Maxim took him to a number of cities, where he aided in the construction of the first electric plants and supervised the installation of lights and wiring.

going to Europe. Mary, in particular, enjoyed the opportunity to walk around and explore her foreign surroundings. Lewis, of course, was busy setting up the first light bulb factory for the English branch of Maxim's business, the Weston Electric Light Company.

Latimer's job was to teach the English workers how to make light bulbs, including how to produce carbon filaments using the process that he had invented. "In nine months time we had the factory in running order," Latimer wrote. Three months ahead of schedule, he completed his assignment and returned to the United States.

But when Latimer got back, there was no job waiting for him. Perhaps because he had returned sooner than expected, he found "every place filled."

Maxim was not one to display excessive loyalty to his employees. Around this time, he wrote an autobiography describing his own success; Lewis Latimer, the man whose inventions and managerial skills had helped build his fortune, was not even mentioned.

Latimer left Maxim's employ in 1883, never to return. Maxim would have cause to regret his arrogant treatment of his brilliant assistant many times in the following years. The name Lewis Latimer would come back to haunt him again and again, for less than a year later Latimer went to work for Maxim's arch rival: Thomas Alva Edison. ✺

7

WORKING FOR
THE WIZARD

❧

The founder of the recording and motion picture as well as the electric light and power industries, Thomas Edison saw a number of people try to capitalize on his many inventions. Latimer, being an expert on patents and electricity, was hired by Edison in 1883 to help protect his interests.

AFTER LEWIS LATIMER left Hiram Maxim's company in 1883, he went to work for the Olmstead Electrical Lighting Company in Brooklyn, New York, as a draftsman and superintendent of lamp construction. While Latimer was employed there, he constructed the Latimer lamp—an example of which has been preserved in the [William] Hammer Historical Collection in New York City. Incredibly, more than 100 years after it was made, the Latimer lamp still works.

The same year that Latimer joined the Olmstead Electrical Lighting Company, his first child was born. On June 12, 1883, after 10 years of marriage, he and Mary became the proud parents of Emma Jeannette. The child would later describe herself as a "baldy" because she had no hair at the time of her birth. Otherwise, she was born a little overweight, with light brown skin, large brown eyes, and a radiant smile. Jeannette was just like her mother, it was said: sweet, charming, and loving.

Fortune soon smiled on the Latimer household again. "After a few months in the Olmstead Electric Company," he recalled, "the Edison people sent for me and I became one of the firm at 65 5th Avenue.

"The Edison United Manufacturing Co." reads the first electric sign ever put into operation. It was installed in about 1888 at 65 5th Avenue in New York City, where Latimer was employed as a draftsman in Thomas Edison's engineering department.

A few months later, I went into the engineering department as draughtsman."

Like most Americans, Latimer knew the story of Thomas Alva Edison's zest for inventing and his rise to widespread fame. It is difficult to overestimate the importance of Edison's contributions to modern civi-

lization, which include the phonograph, the micro-
phone, motion pictures, and the alkaline battery.
Besides devising inventions that changed the world
forever, he vastly improved other existing technology. For example, he was involved in the race to
invent the telephone. Although Bell triumphed in
that contest, Edison subsequently made vast improvements to Bell's invention.

All told, Edison was granted 1,093 patents, a
number that far exceeds any other inventor's total.
His supreme contribution, however, was the electric
light bulb. He not only made the first commercially
practical incandescent lamp, but he designed complete electrical distribution systems for power and
lighting. He understood that light bulbs would be of
little use if electrical power was not readily available.
And to bring power to entire cities, so that every
home could have lights, so that entire factories and
office buildings could be illuminated, a generator far
more powerful than any ever conceived had to be
built—and all the electricity that it created then
needed to be distributed.

Edison proved equal to these tasks. He labored
for long hours at his workshops—themselves the
forerunners of modern, industrial research laboratories—at Menlo Park and West Orange, New Jersey.
And he soon became known as the Wizard of
Menlo Park.

Edison's wizardry was certainly apparent when
it came to the light bulb. An illumination of 25
candlepower—that is, the amount of light equal to
that made by burning 25 candles—is the minimum
amount of light recommended for reading. But before
Edison invented the light bulb, very few homes
enjoyed that much light from candles, kerosene
lamps, or gas lights.

In addition, before Edison harnessed electricity,
public transportation was either by horse or by steam-

Latimer (second from right) poses with the other members of the Edison General Electric Company's legal department in 1894. Two years later, he left his post with the firm to become the chief draftsman of the Board of Patent Control, a governing body created by the Edison General Electric Company and its biggest rival, the Westinghouse Company.

powered trains. Elevators likewise were powered by steam, which could generate only enough power to raise an elevator a few floors. Thus, skyscrapers did not exist until after Edison found a way to distribute electricity.

Edison not only possessed a tremendous intellect but was determined, persistent, and willing to take risks. He had received limited formal schooling, however, and he was often at a loss to understand the mathematical and scientific formulas and equations basic to the work that he did. One aspect of Edison's genius lay in his ability to put together teams of talented individuals who worked with him to turn out the myriad inventions that flowed from his workshops. Edison often played the role of a catalyst with the groups of scientists that he assembled.

As brilliant as Edison was, he made a number of poor business decisions and let several opportunities to grow wealthy from his inventions slip through his fingers. When he did get his hands on money, he spent it faster than it came in. He put the proceeds toward building bigger laboratories, so he could create still more inventions. Between 1879 and 1883, Edison applied for 147 patents in the field of electric lighting.

Edison often had to file amendments to the patents, however, because a number of his applications for a patent were poorly presented. Such was the case with the November 4, 1879, patent application that described the most important parts of his lighting system; it mentioned the use of carbon spirals, which in fact had never worked. Another patent, for a lamp filament, failed to specify what the filament was made of. And in 1883, the U.S. patent commissioner ruled that an Edison rival, William Sawyer, had beaten the Wizard in the race to file a patent for an incandescent lamp with a carbon burner.

Patents clearly played an important role in Edison's work. His Edison Electric Light Company had been founded as a patent-holding company, which meant that the company's success depended on its continued ability to acquire new patents. And the acquisition of patents depended on a detailed knowledge of the process of filing the forms properly at the U.S. Patent Office.

More and more, Edison needed a man such as Latimer. The 35-year-old black inventor knew the patent process inside out and was well versed in electric lighting and power. In addition, he possessed self-discipline, patience, and was attentive to details. Edison had one other reason to be interested in Latimer; his former employer, Hiram Maxim, also happened to be Edison's chief rival.

Latimer quickly justified Edison's faith in him. He tested and checked equipment, and he was put in

A contemporary of Latimer's, inventor Granville Woods became known as the Black Edison because he specialized in the field of electromechanics. Woods was occasionally an adversary of Thomas Edison's, although the two men sometimes worked together.

charge of the company library. But a big part of Latimer's job with the Edison Electric Light Company was to collect information that could be put to use in lawsuits concerning Edison's patents. A number of inventors tried to capitalize on Edison's work without his permission. It was Latimer's role, as an expert on patents and electricity, to set the record straight.

Among the few patent cases that Edison lost were to a black inventor, Granville Woods. Called the

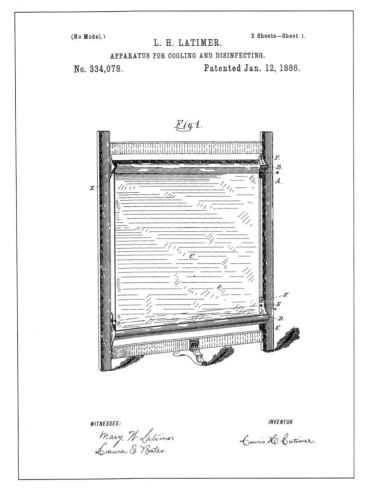

(No Model.)   2 Sheets—Sheet 1.
L. H. LATIMER.
APPARATUS FOR COOLING AND DISINFECTING.
No. 334,078.   Patented Jan. 12, 1886.

Fig. 1.

WITNESSES: INVENTOR
Mary W. Latimer   Lewis H. Latimer.
Laura S. Bates.

This drawing accompanied the patent granted to Latimer on January 12, 1886, for an "Apparatus for Cooling and Disinfecting." Latimer wrote in his application for the patent, "The object of my invention is to present a large evaporating surface for the purpose of cooling the air about or passing over it, or to charge the same with chemical agents . . . to destroy such odors or germs of disease that may exist."

Black Edison by his admirers, Woods, like Latimer, had made himself into a man of science by reading, observing, and experimenting. Like Edison, Woods devised several electrical improvements to the telephone. In all, Woods is credited with more than 50 inventions, including that of railroad telegraphy, which made it possible to transmit messages from one moving train to another. Edison contested Woods for the rights to this invention, but the court ruled in Woods's favor.

Court cases over patent rights fascinated Latimer and kept him busy and learning. Occasionally, he

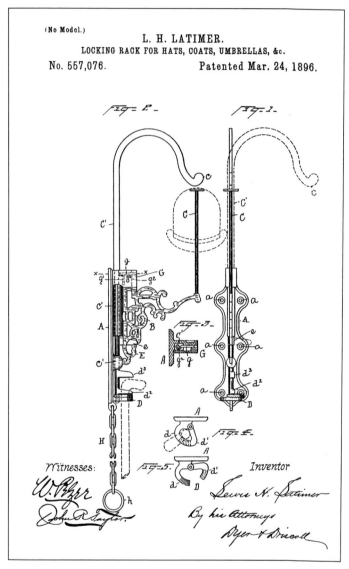

(No Model.)

L. H. LATIMER.
LOCKING RACK FOR HATS, COATS, UMBRELLAS, &c.

No. 557,076.   Patented Mar. 24, 1896.

This drawing accompanied the patent granted to Latimer on March 24, 1896, for a "Locking-rack for Hats, Coats, Umbrellas." Latimer wrote in his patent application, "My invention relates to racks for securely holding hats, coats, umbrellas, and like articles, so that the same may be removed only by the person or persons having a right thereto."

used his impressive linguistic skills to serve Edison, translating articles from French and German into English. (Latimer had taught himself both languages.) Accurate translations were important, for many of the patent cases that Edison was involved in concerned infringement of his rights in Europe.

Not only did Latimer help guide Edison through the patent process, but he was always glad to help

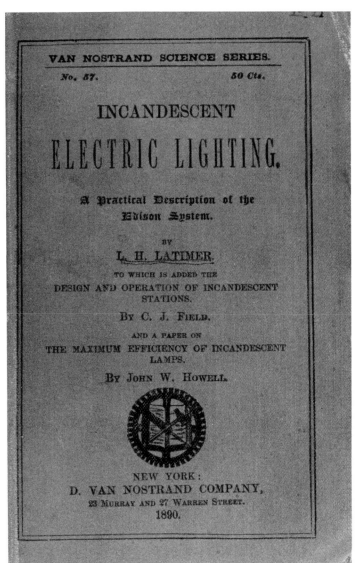

VAN NOSTRAND SCIENCE SERIES.

No. 57.   50 Cts.

INCANDESCENT

ELECTRIC LIGHTING.

A Practical Description of the
Edison System.

BY

L. H. LATIMER.

TO WHICH IS ADDED THE
DESIGN AND OPERATION OF INCANDESCENT
STATIONS.

By C. J. FIELD,

AND A PAPER ON
THE MAXIMUM EFFICIENCY OF INCANDESCENT
LAMPS.

By JOHN W. HOWELL.

NEW YORK:
D. VAN NOSTRAND COMPANY,
23 MURRAY AND 27 WARREN STREET.
1890.

The title page of the book
Incandescent Electric Lighting,
A Practical Description of the
Edison System, *which was*
published in 1890. Thomas Edison
had encouraged Latimer to write
this 140-page account of electric
lighting to help explain the new and
growing field to the public.

other inventors master the procedure that was necessary to obtain a patent. He explained the need of making a drawing of the invention, done to scale, and emphasized the importance of a correctly written description of the invention. Latimer always stressed the importance of patent ownership to new inventors and delighted in patiently detailing the steps of document submission.

Portraits of Latimer's two daughters, Emma Jeannette (above) and Louise Rebecca (opposite page).

Latimer's "Apparatus for Cooling and Disinfecting" patent—which he filed on September 3, 1885, and was approved by the U.S. Patent Office on January 12, 1886—was typical of his work. He designed this device to make rooms cooler and cleaner. The apparatus consisted of a large frame, with a piece of fabric stretched across it, a reservoir at the top of the frame to hold liquid disinfectants, and a drip pan at the bottom to collect any spillover. "The object of my invention," Latimer explained in the patent, "is to present a large evaporating surface for the purpose of cooling the air about or passing over it, or to charge the same with chemical agents . . . to destroy such odors or germs of disease that may exist." The device could be used as a curtain or awning or could be secured to window frames.

Typical of Latimer's subsequent inventions, his "Apparatus for Cooling and Disinfecting" was created to make people's lives safer and more pleasurable. In the years that followed, he would be granted patents for several other inventions, such as "Locking-rack for Hats, Coats, Umbrellas" (U.S. Patent Number 557,076)—designed for use in public places, it was a "simple, efficient, and inexpensive device which will occupy very little space and which can be readily secured in position"—and "A Book Supporter" (U.S. Patent Number 781,890)—to prevent shelved books from getting bent out of shape.

Meanwhile, Latimer continued to be a key member of the Edison Electric Light Company. He was made a draftsman in the engineering department; in 1890, he was transferred to the company's newly created legal department; and he was ultimately named the company's chief draftsman.

The year 1890 also saw D. Van Nostrand & Company publish a 140-page book by Latimer entitled *Incandescent Electric Lighting, A Practical Description of the Edison System*. Edison had encouraged Latimer to write this account, which explained the principles of electric lighting, because the field of electricity was new to the public and was not understood by the average citizen. Latimer's book was so popular that he received a request from the publisher to add more information to the text. Latimer, in turn, asked two of his colleagues, Charles Fields and John Howell, to lend their expertise. Fields wrote about "Design and Operation of Incandescent Stations," and Howell contributed a paper on "The Maximum Efficiency of Incandescent Lamps."

Latimer's description in *Incandescent Electric Lighting* as to how an incandescent lamp produces light attests to his ability to explain a difficult subject to a nonexpert in the field.

> If the electric current can be forced through a substance that is a poor conductor, it will create a degree of heat in that substance, which will be greater or less according to the quality of electricity forced through it. Upon this principle of the heating effect of the electrical current, is based the operation of the incandescent lamp just described. Where copper and platinum wires readily conduct the current, the carbon filament offers a great deal of resistance to its passage, and for this reason becomes very hot, in fact is raised to white heat or incandescence, which gives its name to the lamp. You doubtless wonder why this thread of charcoal is not immediately consumed when in this state, but this is really accounted for when you remember, that without oxygen of the air, there can be no combustion and that every possible trace of air has been removed from the bulb and is so thoroughly sealed up as to prevent admission of the air about it; and yet the lamp does not last forever, for the reason that the action of the current upon the carbon has a tendency to divide up its particles and transfer them from one point to another so that, sooner or later, the filament gives way at some point.

Although the time Latimer spent at work was filled with scientific and technical matters, he used his hours away from the office to cultivate another side of his character. He loved to paint, and he made portraits of family members. He was also a devoted writer—he always seemed to be enriching his life through language in one way or another. He wrote in his journal to record what happened to him and to reflect upon his life, and he wrote poetry to express his deepest emotions.

Latimer's poems bore such titles as "Love Is All," "Praise," "A Happy Life," "Friends," and "Thinking." Some of them spoke of the love that he felt for his wife, such as "The Love Is Like":

> The Love is like the cooling shade of trees
> Or like the fragrant breath of flowers
> My thoughts fly to thee as the wayward bees
> Return to seek again the honeyed flowers.

But Latimer also wrote about his deeper concerns, such as in "The Worker":

> Up in the morning, early
> Before the break of day
> To eat if I had food to eat
> And to my work away.
> When night has spread its shadows
> O'er the country and the town
> I turn my tired feet toward home
> And gladly lie me down,
> And it's day and night and morning
> Through each succeeding year.
> 'Neath the spur of keen necessity
> Or the presence of a fear
> A fear that haunts me ever
> Through each succeeding day
> That those who give the means to live
> May take the means away.

It seems that, try as he might, Latimer remained unable to escape from the same fear that had haunted his father. As capable and successful as Lewis was, he understood that he could still have his livelihood taken away from him, and that everything he had struggled for could vanish. ❧

8

A PIONEER FOR PROGRESS

$\textbf{L}$EWIS LATIMER'S CONCERN for his family's well-being is probably what kept him from making his reunion with his father public knowledge. George Latimer had remained in the Boston area after he had left his family, taking up residence in Lynn, Massachusetts, and working as a paperhanger. He met briefly with Frederick Douglass in the spring of 1894, when the influential black leader came to Boston to give a speech.

Douglass, responding to a letter written by the younger Latimer, recounted his meeting with George Latimer in a letter to Lewis dated September 16.

> Dear Mr. Latimer:
>
> I give you thanks for your excellent letter. It made me proud of you. I was glad to hear of your mother and family. I saw your father for a Moment in Boston, last spring. He seemed in good health then and I am surprised to learn of his condition now. It is fifty two years since I first saw your father and mother in Boston. You can hardly imagine the excitement the attempts to recapture them caused in Boston. It was a new experience for the Abolitionists and they improved it to the full extent of which it was capable.

During this same period, Latimer began to carry on a friendly correspondence with Booker T. Washington, who had founded the Tuskegee Normal and

Latimer is flanked by his wife, Mary, and one of his daughters, Louise, on the porch of their home at 64 Holly Street in Flushing, Queens, a borough of New York City.

A friend of Latimer's, Richard Theodore Greener was the first black American to graduate from Harvard University. He became very active in the fight for black rights and encouraged Latimer to join the battle.

Industrial Institute in Tuskegee, Alabama, in 1881. Working tirelessly over the next decade, Washington built the school into America's largest and best-endowed black educational institution. Meanwhile, he was emerging as a leading spokesman for his race.

Douglass's death on February 20, 1895, cleared the way for a new leader for the black race to come forward. Washington seized the opportunity seven months later, when he delivered his landmark address on racial matters, the Atlanta Compromise. And by the time his second autobiography, *Up from Slavery*, was published in 1901, Washington, like Douglass before him, had lifted himself up from slavery to become the most important black leader in America.

Another person with whom Latimer corresponded regularly was Richard Theodore Greener, the first black American to graduate from Harvard University. A man of considerable intellect, Greener taught philosophy at the University of South Carolina, earned a legal degree and became dean of Howard University's law school, and was appointed to several political offices. He was also very active in the fight for black rights, and he encouraged Latimer to join the battle.

"I am heart and soul in the movement," Latimer wrote back to Greener,

> (1) Because it is necessary that we should show the people of this country that we who have by our martyrdom under the lash; by our heroism on the battlefield; by our Christian forbearance beneath an overwhelming burden of injustice; and by our submission to the laws of the native land, proven ourselves worthy citizens of our common country.
>
> (2) Because there is no separation of the colored Americans from those of the white American, and it is our duty to show our country, and . . . the world that we are looking to the interests of the country at large, when we protest against the crime and injustice meted out to any class or conditions of our citizens.
>
> (3) Because the community which permits a crime against its humblest member to go unpunished is nursing into life

and strength a power which will ultimately threaten its own existence.

(4) Because our history conclusively proves that the attempt to degrade any portion, class, or race of our common people has always been fraught with more danger to the oppressor than the oppresed.

(5) Because an evenhanded justice to all, under and through the law, is the only safe course to pursue for where might makes right, brute strength will supersede intelligence in the control of our communities.

Latimer strongly supported the idea of a national convention of black Americans, believing that it would give greater voice to the black cause. "We should have a National Convention," he told Greener,

and if that Convention, forgetting all other considerations directs its energies to presenting its cause before the people, as it affects the people at large, presenting it as our fathers did the question of slavery, with facts and figures, showing, as it can be shown, that where the Colored American is lynched, the white American is assassinated; that ignorance and crime go hand in hand with prejudice; that schools and churches multiply where there is neither class nor color distinctions in the law; that class legislation puts a premium on ignorance and illiteracy, in that it aids a man to think himself superior by accident of birth than by the achievements of merit and ability. If our cause be made the common cause, and all our claims and demands be founded on justice and humanity, recognizing that we must wrong no man in winning OUR rights, I have faith to believe that the Nation will respond to our plea for equality before the law, security under the law, and an opportunity, by and through maintenance of the law, to enjoy with our fellow citizens of all races and complexions the blessings guaranteed us under the Constitution, of "life, liberty, and the pursuit of happiness."

Those guarantees of "life, liberty, and the pursuit of happiness" were being sorely tested. In 1868, five years after the Emancipation Proclamation legally ended slavery in the South, the Fourteenth Amendment was ratified. The amendment was designed to assure newly freed blacks the same legal rights and

Latimer (front row, left) poses for a family portrait during the early 1920s, with Gerald Latimer Norman (back row, far left), Jeannette Latimer Norman (back row, third from left), Gerald F. Norman (back row, center), Louise Latimer (back row, second from right), Winifred Latimer Norman (back row, far right), and Mary Wilson Latimer (front row, center).

privileges as whites. But the United States Supreme Court, with its celebrated 1896 decision in the case *Plessy v. Ferguson*, changed all that.

Plessy began when a black man, Homer Adolph Plessy, refused to ride in the blacks-only car of a train passing through Louisiana. Charged with violating a state law that required racial segregation in public facilities, Plessy was convicted by Ferguson, a Louisiana judge. Plessy's lawyer argued before the Supreme Court that enforced separation of the two races violated the Fourteenth Amendment, which guarantees all citizens "the equal protection of the laws." The Supreme Court upheld the Louisiana segregation law, ruling that separate but "equal" facilities satisfied the amendment's "equal protection" guarantee.

Although the Supreme Court's decision technically applied only to Louisiana law, it opened the gates for a flood of new Jim Crow laws—statutes that required racial separation in both private residential areas and public facilities. And by 1900, blacks in many states found themselves restricted to Jim Crow drinking fountains, railroad cars, movie theater sections, hospitals, and schools. Despite the *Plessy* ruling, few state or local governments enforced the equality of the institutions and services available to blacks.

Latimer did what he could—in his own quiet way. In 1902, for example, he expressed his concern over the lack of a black representative on the Brooklyn School Board in a letter to New York City mayor Seth Low. Then Latimer collected 300 names on a petition calling for a black member on the board, S. R. Scottron. Latimer sent the petition to the mayor with the following note:

> Since you represent ALL the people in this city, and since all races and nationalities forming part of this heterogeneous citizenship have their due consideration from the appointmenting powers, Mr. S.R. Scottron, be considered. Not alone as our representative, but as a good citizen, a worthy gentleman, and one whose influence in his native city warrants the assertion that he would be a bit representative of any of her people, regardless of racial differences.

Latimer also did work on behalf of the local immigrant community. In 1906, he volunteered his services to the Henry Street Settlement House, a group that provided immigrants with job training and health care. Latimer taught English as well as mechanical drawing to a number of the immigrants who took advantage of the settlement house.

By then, Latimer and his family were living in a two-and-a-half-story frame house at 64 Holly Street

A certificate presented to Latimer's granddaughter, Winifred Latimer Norman, in honor of his work at the Henry Street Settlement House in New York City. Latimer taught English and mechanical drawing to the immigrants at the settlement house.

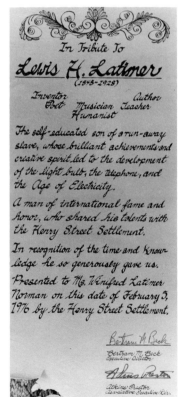

One of the many drawings that Latimer did during his leisure time. This one is entitled Greek Beggar.

in Flushing, located in the New York City borough of Queens. A second daughter, Louise Rebecca, had joined the clan in 1890, and she tended to be frank in her relations with people, unlike her quiet, older sister, Jeannette. Life in the Latimer household was that of a happy, devoted, cultured, and civic-minded family. Friends from Brooklyn, where the Latimers had previously lived, traveled by trolley car on Sundays to spend a day with the family.

Visitors were treated to the charm and exquisite cooking of Mary Latimer, who sometimes showcased her musical talents. Jeannette, who studied at the Institute of Musical Art in New York City—and later at Julliard—also treated the guests to her artistry at the piano. She became a concert pianist, piano teacher, and composer. (Louise went on to study art at Pratt Institute and later became an artist.) Among the visitors to the Latimer household were James Weldon Johnson and his brother, Rosamond, who were then a highly successful songwriting team; in the following decade, Johnson would switch careers and become the first black to head the National Association for the Advancement of Colored People (NAACP). Another occasional guest was W. E. B. Du Bois, the noted scholar and activist who became editor of the NAACP's influential publication, the *Crisis*.

Latimer's various activities and family obligations kept him busy indeed. But his work for Thomas Edison remained the focal point of his daily life. Back in 1889, the Edison Electric Light Company had combined with his other businesses to become the Edison General Electric Company. Seven years later, it joined forces with one of its competitors, the Westinghouse Company, to form the Board of Patent Control in an effort to avoid costly legal battles between the two companies. Latimer promptly switched jobs, going from his post with the Edison General Electric Company's legal department to the Board of Patent Control. He became the board's chief draftsman, and he held this position until 1911, when the board was abolished. ❧

9

"HE WAS
A RENAISSANCE MAN"

"Which way will he fall?" Latimer wrote at the bottom of this 1912 illustration, which he entitled My Situation. *At the time, he was working as a consulting engineer for a firm headed by Edwin Hammer, a patent lawyer and engineer.*

PATENT LAWYER AND engineer Edwin Hammer had been the chief technical assistant of the Board of Patent Control. Along with his brother William, who was employed by Thomas Edison and had masterminded the promotion of many of his inventions, Edwin was quite familiar with Lewis Latimer's contributions to the electric industry. In 1911, shortly after the board disbanded, Latimer was asked to become a patent consultant for Edwin Hammer's firm.

By this time, Latimer was 63 years old and not in the best of health. Vision problems had been plaguing him for much of the past two decades. Nevertheless, he continued his association with Hammer's company until 1922, when his career as an electrical engineer came to an end as his eyesight began to fail. He received a pension from the Edison General Electric Company of $17.50 a week, which was supplemented by a pension from the military of $72 per month.

Meanwhile, William Hammer had already seen to it that Latimer and his colleagues in the Edison organization would retain their place in history. For one thing, Hammer, acting as the unofficial historian of the Edison organization, amassed the most complete collection of incandescent lamps and electric light devices in the nation. And on February 11, 1918, Edison's 71st birthday, Hammer chose to mark the occasion by bringing together the 28 charter members of the Edison organization. Latimer was part of this select group, which became known as the Edison Pioneers. Thereafter, each year, on Edison's birthday, they would convene either at the Menlo Park laboratory or in nearby Newark. Latimer, according to his journal, always took part in these gatherings.

Another type of celebration took place in 1923, when Lewis and Mary Latimer toasted their 50th wedding anniversary and were showered with hundreds of telegrams, cards, and letters from their loving family members and friends. By then, Lewis and Mary were grandparents. In 1911, Jeannette married Gerald Norman, a high school teacher from the island of Jamaica, with whom she had two children,

Latimer (front row, second from left) stands proudly with the other Edison Pioneers in honoring Thomas Edison (second row, eighth from left) in Orange, New Jersey, on the occasion of the noted inventor's 73rd birthday. Founded two years earlier, the Edison Pioneers assembled every February 11, the date of Edison's birth.

Latimer (left) and the Grand Army of the Republic (GAR) present an American flag to P.S. 24 in Flushing, New York. He was an officer in the organization, which was made up of former Union soldiers and sailors.

Gerald and Winifred Latimer Norman. A doting grandfather, Lewis Latimer took great delight in his grandchildren.

Latimer also instilled in them strong religious and social beliefs. He had been a founding member of a Unitarian church in Flushing. He also belonged to the Grand Army of the Republic (GAR), an organization consisting of former Union soldiers and sailors. As an officer in the GAR, he strove to keep alive the memory of fallen comrades, lobbied the U.S. government for pension benefits for veterans, and worked to educate children about the Civil War.

Mary Latimer fell ill in the months that followed her 50th wedding anniversary, and she finally succumbed to her illness in 1924. Her husband laid her body to rest in the Oak Grove Cemetery, near her birthplace in Fall River, Massachusetts. It would become his own grave site as well.

The death of his wife and a stroke that left one side of his body paralyzed sent Latimer into a deep state of depression. In an attempt to cheer him up, his family and friends selected some of the hundreds of poems he had written, had them printed on handmade Italian paper, and had them bound as a book, *The Poems of Love and Life*. Fifty copies were printed, and they were presented to him on September 14, 1925, on the occasion of his 77th birthday.

Lewis Latimer died three years later, on December 11, 1928. The Edison Pioneers were among those who paid tribute to Latimer, issuing a statement that said in part:

> He was of the colored race, the only one in our organization, and was one of those to respond to the initial call that led to the formation of the Edison Pioneers, January 24, 1918. Broadmindedness, versatility in the accomplishment of things intellectual and cultural, a linguist, a devoted husband and father, all were characteristic of him. His genial presence will be missed from our gatherings.

Additional tributes would follow more than a half-century later. In the mid-1970s, the Henry Ford Museum in Dearborn, Michigan, displayed an exhibit that highlighted Latimer's contributions to science and industry; the exhibit included some of Latimer's lamps from William Hammer's collection. On September 10, 1982, a large crowd gathered along 34th Avenue in Flushing to witness a public ceremony that

A selection of Latimer's poetry was published in Poems of Love and Life, *a handsomely bound book that his family arranged to have printed in 1925.*

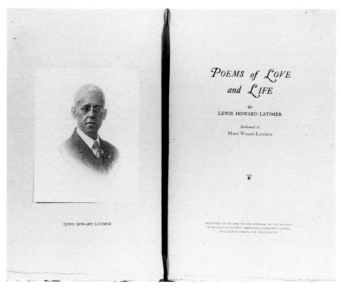

The Latimer clan in Bridgeport, Connecticut: (from left to right) grandson Gerald Latimer Norman; daughter Emma Jeannette Latimer Norman; Lewis Latimer; brother George and his wife; and granddaughter Winifred Latimer Norman.

culminated in part of the street being renamed Latimer Place. And in 1984, the Edison National Historic Site in West Orange, New Jersey, honored Latimer by displaying such items as his patents, his published book of poetry, and other memorabilia. A bust of Latimer was also part of the exhibit.

Four years later, under the headline "It Was a Moving Spectacle!", the *New York Times* described an event that had brought reporters and television camera crews to Flushing. On the morning of December 13, 1988, spectators lined up along a section of the area's quiet, snow-covered streets to watch workers loosen Latimer's home at 64 Holly Street from its foundation and rig it securely onto the flatbed of a huge truck. The 100-year-old frame house had been scheduled to be demolished; several smaller homes were to be built in its place.

A group of citizens had formed the Committee to Save the Latimer House and had launched a crusade to raise funds for the preservation of the historic house. Leading the way were Latimer's two grandchildren: Gerald Latimer Norman, a prominent administrative law judge in Brooklyn, and Winifred Latimer

NEW YORK, NEW JERSEY, CONNECTICUT / SATURDAY, AUGUST 6, 1988

A Campaign to Remember an Inventor

By JOSEPH P. FRIED

For the last 20 years of his life, Lewis H. Latimer, a black inventor and major pioneer in the development of electric lighting, lived in a comfortable two-and-a-half-story frame house in Flushing, Queens.

Now, 60 years after his death, the house is scheduled to be demolished so that several new homes can be built on its quiet, well kept block. But Mr. Latimer's descendants and people concerned with Queens history and with black history have another idea.

Working against time, they have begun a campaign to save the gabled white house by moving it from its site, at 137-53 Holly Avenue, to another location in Flushing a mile away, on a city-owned athletic field at Leavitt Street and 34th Avenue. They would then like to turn the house into a museum whose exhibits would illuminate the life and achievements not only of Mr. Latimer — the son of a former slave who became a leading electrical engineer — but of other black scientists as well.

"He was an extraordinary man and achieved a great deal in the field of science," said Tom Lloyd, co-chairman of a committee trying to raise the $36,000 needed to move the Latimer house. Mr. Latimer, who was born in Chelsea, Massachusetts, was 80 when he died in 1928.

Mr. Latimer helped make electric lighting practical by devising in the 1880's a light bulb filament — the slender wire that the current heats to incandescence — that was longer-lasting than previous filaments. He also oversaw the installation of electric lighting in streets and buildings in New York City, Philadelphia, London and other cities, and was associated at various times with Thomas A. Edison and with Alexander Graham Bell, for whom, as a self-taught young draftsman, he made the patent drawings for the telephone.

"There are very few houses related to black people designated as landmarks in New York City and State," said Mr. Lloyd, director of the Store Front Mu-

Continued on Page 29, Column 4

The New York Times/Sara Krulwich

Winifred Latimer Norman, the granddaughter of Lewis H. Latimer, outside the inventor's home, which is scheduled for demolition, in Flushing, Queens.

A featured article in the New York Times in 1988 recounts Winifred Latimer Norman's effort to save her grandfather's home in Queens from demolition. The house was eventually transported to nearby Leavitt Field, to be converted into a museum honoring the inventor and electric-lighting pioneer.

Norman, an internationally known church leader, social worker, and public speaker. The two children of Jeannette Latimer had spent many happy hours in their grandfather's house and were determined to let the world know more about the scientific genius who had played a part in revolutionizing modern society.

The other members of the Committee to Save the Latimer House worked diligently with Gerald and Winifred Latimer Norman to preserve the house. Their efforts were aided by the Queens Historical

Society, which took a deep interest in not only preserving the dwelling but turning it into a museum. The Lewis H. Latimer Fund, Inc. is responsible for restoring the house. The museum will offer a variety of exhibitions, including one that will show how the inside of a light bulb works, and information about career options in science will be made available.

Claire Schulman, the Queens borough president, announced at a public gathering, "A museum and an educational center will be established in the Lewis H. Latimer House to remind people for generations to come about how black Americans broke the shackles of slavery and went on to make major contributions to the growth and development of our nation and society."

In addition to citing examples of Latimer's accomplishments, Schulman said, "Thomas Alva Edison invented the light bulb, but it was Lewis Latimer who developed and improved the filament that made electric lighting practical. Alexander Graham Bell invented the telephone, but it was Lewis who did the patent drawings that made its production possible. While the names of Edison and Bell are known to the everyday school child, Lewis Latimer, like many other people of color, has been denied his rightful place in history."

And so the Latimer house was saved. To prepare for the moving of the house, electrical and cable crews dismantled overhead wires to make room for the house to move down the broad city streets. Trees were pruned. Traffic was rerouted. The local school children were permitted to leave their classrooms to witness the event, which had the air of a grand patriotic parade. "I never saw a house moving before," observed a third-grader who watched the spectacle.

The Latimer house, firmly secured to the flatbed truck, moved slowly along Holly Street and did not reach its destination until shortly before 1 P.M.:

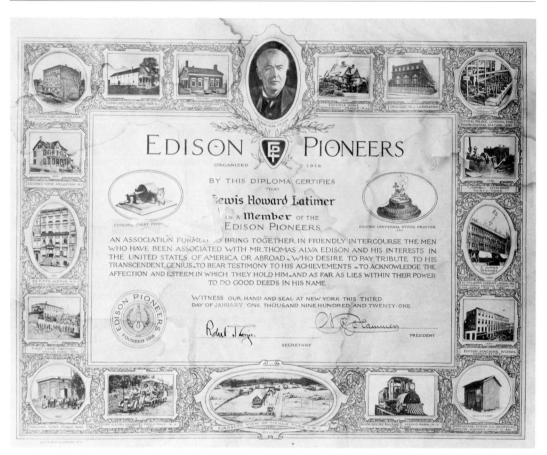

This diploma was presented to Latimer, certifying that he was a member of the Edison Pioneers, "an association formed to bring together in friendly intercourse the men who have been associated with Mr. Thomas Alva Edison and his interests in the United States of America or abroad." Latimer was one of the association's charter members.

Leavitt Field, a city-owned athletic field located at Leavitt Street and 34th Avenue in Queens. A block away was a housing development known as Latimer Gardens.

The local residents held a grand celebration to acknowledge the arrival of the inventor's home. The Youth Council, a group of teenagers who lived in Latimer Gardens, made a pledge to watch over the house until it could be set on a new foundation. Each member of the council received a T-shirt with the words "Lewis H. Latimer House Council Protector" printed on it.

At a formal ceremony to dedicate the old home to its new purpose—the museum is scheduled to open in 1995—Winifred Latimer Norman read one of the verses written by her grandfather and printed in *The Poems of Love and Life*. "He was a Renaissance man," Norman said to her audience with obvious pride. And then she reminded her listeners that in addition to writing the first book to explain Edison's electric light, Lewis Latimer was also a poet, a musician, and an artist. ❧

CHRONOLOGY

—— ❦ ——

1848   Lewis Howard Latimer born in Chelsea, Massachusetts on September 4

1861   Begins working as an office boy for Isaac Wright, a prominent lawyer

1864   Joins the U.S. Navy

1865   Hired by the patent-lawyer firm of Crosby and Gould as an office boy

1873   Marries Mary Wilson on September 20

1874   Patents an improvement on train water closets with W. C. Brown

1876   Executes the drawings for Alexander Graham Bell's patent for the telephone

1879   Begins working for Hiram Maxim's U.S. Electric Lighting Company; invents a carbon filament to make electric lights longer lasting and more affordable

1882   Receives a patent for arc lamps; travels to Philadelphia, New York, and Montreal to supervise the installation of lights and wiring; sets up a light-bulb factory in London

1883   Daughter Emma Jeannette born; Latimer constructs the Latimer lamp while at the Olmstead Electrical Lighting Company; begins working for Thomas Alva Edison

1886   Latimer receives patent for "Apparatus for Cooling and Disinfecting" on January 12

1890   Named Edison Electric Light Company's chief draftsman; publishes *Incandescent Electric Lighting, A Practical Description of the Edison System*; daughter Louise Rebecca born

1896   Becomes the chief draftsman at the Board of Patent Control; receives patent for "Locking-rack for Hats, Coats, Umbrellas" on March 24

1911   Becomes a patent consultant at Edwin Hammer's firm

1918   Becomes a charter member of the Edison Pioneers

1925   *The Poems of Love and Life* is published

1928   Dies on December 11

1988   Latimer's home in Flushing, New York, is moved to a new location in Queens to serve as a museum

FURTHER READING
〄

Adler, David A. *Thomas Alva Edison: A Great Inventor*. New York: Holiday House, 1990.

Burt, McKinley. *Black Inventors of America*. Portland, OR: National Book Company, 1989.

Cosner, Shaaron. *The Light Bulb*. New York: Walker, 1984.

Donovan, Richard X. *Black Scientists of America*. Portland, OR: National Book Company, 1990.

Haber, Louis. *Black Pioneers of Science and Invention*. San Diego: Harcourt Brace Jovanovich, 1991.

Haskins, James. *Outward Dreams: Black Inventors and their Inventions*. New York: Walker, 1991.

Hayden, Robert C. *Eight Black American Inventors*. Reading, MA: Addison-Wesley, 1972.

James, Portia P. *The Real McCoy: African American Invention and Innovation*. Washington, D.C: Anacostia Museum/Smithsonian Institution, 1989.

Klein, Aaron E. *The Hidden Contributors: Black Scientists and Inventors in America*. Garden City, NY: Doubleday, 1971.

Russell, Sharman Apt. *Frederick Douglass*. New York: Chelsea House, 1988.

Turner, Glennette Tilley. *Lewis Howard Latimer*. Englewood Cliffs, NJ: Silver Burdett, 1991.

Van Sertima, Ivan, ed. *Blacks in Science: Ancient and Modern*. New Brunswick, NJ: Transaction Books, 1984.

INDEX

PICTURE CREDITS

———— ❧ ————

NATHAN IRVIN HUGGINS, one of America's leading scholars in the field of black studies, helped select the titles for the BLACK AMERICANS OF ACHIEVEMENT series, for which he also served as senior consulting editor. He was the W.E.B. Du Bois Professor of History and of Afro-American Studies at Harvard University and the director of the W.E.B. Du Bois Institute for Afro-American Research at Harvard. He received his doctorate from Harvard in 1962 and returned there as a professor in 1980 after teaching at Columbia University, the University of Massachusetts, Lake Forest College, and the California State University, Long Beach. He was the author of four books and dozens of articles, including *Black Odyssey: The Afro-American Ordeal in Slavery*, *The Harlem Renaissance*, and *Slave and Citizen: The Life of Frederick Douglass*, and was associated with the Children's Television Workshop, National Public Radio, the Boston Athenaeum, the Museum of Afro-American History, the Howard Thurman Educational Trust, and Upward Bound. Professor Huggins died in 1989, at the age of 62, in Cambridge, Massachusetts.

WINIFRED LATIMER NORMAN, granddaughter of Lewis Latimer, is a retired social worker who lives in New York City. She holds an honorary doctorate in humane letters from the Meadville-Lombard Theological School in Chicago and is vice-president of the Lewis H. Latimer Fund, Inc., the organization dedicated to making Latimer's home into a museum.

LILY PATTERSON is a curriculum specialist for library services with the Department of Education in Baltimore, Maryland, where she lives. She is the author of nearly 20 books for juveniles.